4Ms

Muted Molestation that Manifested Mentally

Trimika Cooper, *Visionary Author*

Co Authored By:

Sharmane Burch, Ursula Jones, Claudia Massey, Marcus Solomon

Printed in the United States of America.

ISBN: 979-8-9876649-3-3
Edited, Formatted and Published by Empower Her Publishing, LLC
empowerherpublishing.com

Table of Contents

Introduction

Research shows that more than 90% of abusers are people children know, love and trust. Additionally, 30-40% of victims are abused by a family member and 50% are abused by someone outside the family whom they know and trust. The signs of sexual abuse are not always present and many children do not report that they have been sexually abused, not even to their parents. While these may seem like only statistics to some, they are a gruesome reality for others.

In this book, five authors give you a front row seat to their personal trauma associated with childhood abuse. They make the statistics very much real as they recount the daunting, malicious encounters with the predators of their pasts. They have survived the season of shame and boarded the voyage of victory as they celebrate bravery and survivorship. No longer are they bound by the chains of silence that held them down. Finally, they have been unmuted and are ready to share their truths.

4Ms: Muted Molestation that Manifested Mentally was written to not only free the overcomers who are included herein, but to also free the little girl or boy who is still hiding within the one whose tears will shed from reading a story which sounds all too familiar. It was written to encourage parents to take a step back and be present with their children in an effort to recognize the signs of abuse.

Childhood abuse is a generational cycle of unaddressed behavior. It's time to stand up and speak out against childhood molestation. It's time to unmute!

Foreword

Trimika Cooper

Countless nights of waking up to a raging monstrous hurricane can never be settling to a child. Plates breaking, shoes and other household items flying. My mother is screaming and crying, fighting for her life and ours. My sister and I endured this often. The damage this hurricane left in our home was life altering. I can remember one morning when the hurricane emerged, my mother told us to get up and get under the kitchen table to hide from the debris whirling around the room. I could smell the aroma of chicken noodle soup. "Stop calling me out my name in front of my kids," my mother told the hurricane. It kept regurgitating foul items from its core. My mother advised the hurricane to stop but it refused to restrain. The piercing howl that came from the hurricane after my mother threw that scalding pot of chicken noodle soup in its face was astonishing. From the onset of the noodles sticking to the center, it began to fester with boils and blisters. As my mom got us up from under the table, she told us to run to Aunt Mae's house. Aunt Mae was the neighborhood auntie all the kids loved. She would help any and every one in time of need. The streets of North Philly were rough, especially for us not having any family that I knew of that lived there. As we knocked on Aunt Mae's door at the crack of dawn, she let us in and didn't ask any questions.

Staying with Aunt Mae was great. She made sure we ate as a family at the table, bathed, did our hair and went to school daily. But what she didn't know was that I was being molested in the room right beside her. Hell, I didn't even know I was being molested at that time. I slept in the bed with another little girl who was ten years old and I was eight. She was a nice girl in the beginning, showing me the ropes around Aunt Mae's home. She had been there for a while. Aunt Mae was caring for other children in addition to my sister and me. You could say it was a foster home, but she wasn't state approved. She was just an older woman who didn't mind helping families in need. My first week there was good, and I became comfortable, but wanted to be home with my mom. I would cry at night wondering if that hurricane killed her. My roommate would comfort me and tell me everything was going to be alright and that I was so pretty and light skinned. I never understood what she meant by that. It started with her rubbing my back which I thought was harmless because she was trying to make me feel better. As time went by, she would tell me we were going to play a game she and her sister used to play. So when we went to bed she would rub on her breasts and tell me to do the same to make them grow. We would laugh and then she told me I was doing it wrong. She began to massage my nipples to show me how it was supposed to be done, and again, stated that I was so pretty and light skinned. My mother never talked to me about inappropriate touching, but at this point, I started to think something wasn't right. I told her I didn't feel right doing this. She would reply, "It's ok because I'm not a boy. You're not supposed to let boys touch you." Since she was older, I figured she was right.

As we came to the end of another school week, I can remember my mom coming to see us. Aunt Mae told her to come upstairs first. From the look of her grotesque face, I knew she got in the path of that hurricane again. Aunt Mae put makeup on her to make her look more presentable. I cried when she left. She told us she would be back soon to get us to come back home. That night after taking a bath, I cried even more thinking about how my mom looked. I knew she was in pain and danger. My roommate told me everything was going to be ok. She laid beside me and began to rub my breasts and started to suck them, telling me she was going to make me feel better. I told her no. I didn't feel right. She was a nice girl but had a mean streak as well. Being that she was the oldest there, we all looked up to her. She would say, "well I'm not your friend and don't talk to me" when she didn't get her way. Then she would hit or pinch me. How could I not talk to her? She was my only friend there and I didn't like being hit. It made me think of the hurricane hitting my mother. So I said "alright" and let her do it. She started to put her finger on my vagina attempting to put it inside. It hurt me so bad. At the time I just knew it hurt, but as an adult and now knowing my female anatomy, I realize she didn't know where the opening was. She commenced to put her mouth on my vagina. She would look at me and repeat, "you're so pretty," as she continued to give me oral sex. After she was done, she would tell me to go wash up. I didn't know how I should feel, but I didn't say anything because I was too scared she would hit me. After that night, she would perform oral sex on me almost every night and to be honest, I began to like the way it felt.

After about three months, my mom came and got us and to my surprise, had escaped the hurricane. I missed my mother so much and was so glad to be back with her. We packed up and moved back to North Carolina. I thought my mom was staying with us but she just brought us to live with our grandparents. I didn't have a problem with that because I would much rather be with my grandparents than dealing with the hurricane. I always wondered what happened to my roommate. I didn't miss her but I did miss the oral sex. Over the years, I have done research and found that one in four girls and one in six boys will be sexually abused before the age of 18. I didn't know I was sexually abused until I found out what it was. Being told that I was pretty became something everyone would tell me growing up. I disliked hearing it so much to the point I would put baby oil on my body and lay on my grandparents' back porch in the sun to tan, hoping I would turn dark skinned like my dad. Who wouldn't want someone to tell them that they're pretty? Those simple words would leave a lifelong scab no one could see but me.

Fast forward to the age of maybe 11, I can remember staying overnight with a friend. We had so much fun during the day playing, climbing trees, and picking grapes. I had forgotten all about the oral sex I used to receive until one night her older sister asked me to sleep with her. She had to be 18, but I didn't think anything of it. I got in the bed with her and she began to tell me that we were going to do something her and her best friend did all the time. She pulled my underwear off and began to give me oral sex. And to my astonishment, the first thing she said was, “you’re so pretty.” I immediately thought about my first encounter having this happen to me. But this time was different because she told me to do it to her. I said “no, I don’t know how to.” She said, “I will tell you what to do.” So I put my head under the cover and got close to her vagina. I had never seen someone else's private area, especially up close and personal like this. It was hairy and it smelled really musty, like onions. Just the smell alone made me gag. There was no way I was going to do it. I told her, “NO, I can’t.” I thought she was going to hit me but she didn’t. She just said, “ok you can go back to my sister's room now.” I was relieved as I went back to my friend's room. She was asleep when I got in there so I didn’t have to explain what I was doing back. I felt so uncomfortable the next day and I was ready to go back home. You never know what goes on in someone else's home.

As I began to hit puberty, I felt like I needed that attention guys and girls gave me. The old folk would say I was a fast tail gal, but I had been screaming for years and NOBODY ever heard me. I wasn’t fast. I wasn't sexually active yet, but I loved the attention. At an early age, I realized I could get a lot of what I wanted just by talking to someone because I WAS PRETTY! As time went by, my body began to change. My breasts began to grow at an unbelievably fast rate. I had already started my menstrual cycle and my mind was consumed with so much anger, unanswered questions, and I didn't know why. Living with my grandmother was great but I wanted to be with my mom. I wanted to talk to her and ask her questions I had about how I was feeling. There was a void in my life and for a while, I thought it was my mom, but that was not it. There was an aching feeling that I had been having for quite some time. I wanted it to stop but I didn't know how to make it cease or even what it really was.

By the time I reached the 8th grade, that ache that I had finally went away until one day when I came home from school. A family friend, who was also our maintenance guy, was at our house fixing our back door. He was an older guy, probably older than my dad. I went to the bathroom as I always do when I get home. As I came out of the bathroom and entered my room to put my backpack down, he came in, grabbed me and put me on my bed. He had a tight grip on my wrist with one hand and put the other hand over my mouth. As he held the one hand over my mouth, one of his fingers was blocking my nostrils and I was having trouble breathing. I was so scared but he told me I better not scream. My grandma and sister were outside on the front porch. My body was shaking and I started to cry. He pulled my shirt and bra up and started sucking on one of my breasts. He sucked so hard my nipple felt like he was biting it. I had tears running in my ears as he laid on my small frame body. He was excited as he put his hand between my legs and rubbed my vagina vigorously as he whispered, "you are so pretty." OMG! There were those words again and my mind went back to my first encounter. I could feel a bulge growing in his pants and he started to breathe rapidly. I laid on that bed and began to pray: "God please let my grandma come in here and catch this man." Who would have thought this old man would ever do something like this? My grandmother trusted him in our home and around the family. He was no stranger, more like an uncle to us. Something seemed to startle him and he jumped up and pulled my shirt down and said, "You better not tell anyone, especially Blanch because it would kill her." I ran in the bathroom and cried. I took a washcloth and put it over my mouth to muffle my scream. I was still shaking and my knees were unstable. I couldn't believe this had just happened in my own home.

After that last encounter, I'm not sure what happened to me but I had a horrible attitude. I was always angry and I felt someone owed me something. Who or what they owed me, I don't know. I began to feel that void again. I started to question my sexuality. Am I gay or bisexual? Those were the questions I asked God and myself. Even though I was young, I knew God. My grandmother made sure we went to church so I also knew how to pray. Somehow, going to church and praying still didn't change the way I felt or the void I was feeling. As a result, I became a big flirt and started talking to guys older than me. I ended up having sex with a guy who was 18 and I was 14. It was my first time having vaginal penetration. I got pregnant with my first child my first time. After having my child, I began to think about the things I went through growing up and I vowed that I would try my best to protect my children so they would never go through the same things I did. This was especially important since I now had a little girl. Having a child makes you look at things in a different perspective. I now have four children and I tried to shelter them as they grew up because I was afraid someone would molest them. I always wanted to tell my parents about my encounters but never got a chance to before they passed away. I always talked to my children about their body parts and that no one should touch them in any inappropriate way and to never keep secrets from momma. I didn't allow them to sit in any man's lap or get tickled by anyone. My girls would always ask if they could spend the night at a friend's house and I would always say no. I lived in fear of someone hurting my children. I still have issues that I deal with from being molested and muted for years. Now that I work with children professionally, I'm a big advocate of child molestation. I pray this book helps someone who may be going through or have already gone through similar situations.

Trimika Cooper *is from Chadbourn, NC, but is a resident of Charlotte, NC where she lives with her husband, Genatus Cooper. She is the mother of four children: Sharmane, Destinee, Marcus, and Jayden, grandmother to three granddaughters: Amina, Angel, and Anissa and also has a fur baby named Grace. She is an ordained minister who loves helping those in need. Trimika is also an Assistant Director at Harris Learning Academy, CEO of Cooper's Creative Stylez Balloon Décor, Faith Family & Fabulous Hair T-shirt line, Co-Author of Amazon's #1 Best-Selling book, Reclaiming My Life, which has a Podcast on YouTube, and Co-Author of the forthcoming The Final Chapter: Reclaiming My Life After the Storm.*

Facebook: Min Trimika Cooper
Facebook: Cooper's Creative Stylez
Instagram: Coopers_ Creative_ Stylez

Acknowledgments

Tonya Featherson
TASK Enterprise Printing and Design, LLC
www.taskenterpriseprintinganddesign.com
Facebook:
https://www.facebook.com/taskenterprise?mibextid=ZbWKwL
Instagram:
@task_enterprise_printing_2896

Patricia Finney
Trinity Creations
Facebook: Patricia Finney
Instagram: pfinney0316
LinkedIn: Patricia Finney

Shapora Faulk
Facebook: Shapora Faulk

LoWanda Davis
LoWanda Davis Productions LLC
www.ldavisproductions.com
Facebook: LoWanda Dee Davis

Instagram: @dee2davis
linkedin.com/in/lowanda-davis-14382010

Laura Harris
Harris Learning Academy
6141 Statesville Rd., Charlotte, NC 28269
704-921-1153
ChildcareCharlotte.com

Troubling Times

Sharmane Burch

When I was a child, my mom would take me to the babysitter's house. This was not an ordinary babysitter; she was an older lady who kept kids. She was so sweet and loved everyone, so parents felt comfortable leaving their children with her. I had been going to her since I was a baby. She had two grandchildren who lived with her. Her granddaughter and I were the same age and we became great friends through the years. One particular day my mom dropped me off at the place she thought was safe. Little did she know, I was being molested by the babysitter's grandson who was 14 or 15 years old at the time. From the time I was five years old, he would make me perform oral sex on him every day when he came home from school. His sister knew about it and she would try to hide me in her closet and put cover over me, but he would find me every time. In her attempt to save me, my friend hid me in their outdoor garage one day. Her brother was so upset that he broke her

Barbie doll head off until I came out. We never told anyone because he threatened to kill my family if we did and I believed him.

The abuse went on until I was 13 until the last time was the last time. On this particular day, he had gone out with some friends and his sister and I were glad that we could finally have fun together without him being around. We took turns playing his Nintendo 64 in his room and it was my turn. She left the room and he walked in while I was playing and sat behind me. At 13 years old, my body was fully matured. As he sat behind me, he lifted my shirt and started licking my back then proceeded to rub my breasts. I quickly jumped up and went to his sister's room and started crying. She sat next to me and asked, "He did it again?" I nodded yes and she replied, "We need to tell someone." I waited until I got to my grandma's house and I told her. She called my mom and stepdad and they quickly reacted. My stepdad wanted to kill him. They asked me what I wanted to happen to him and I said I didn't want anything to happen because I forgive him. I just wanted it to stop. I know many may wonder why I didn't want him locked up for what he had done for so many years. Well, I felt like the damage was already done and that God would handle him as well as me for forgiving him. My parents and grandma went to his grandma's house to talk to his parents about the situation. They had him leave the house for his safety, because emotions were high and my family was hurt, especially since this was supposed to be a safe environment for me. His mom was crying and kept saying she was so sorry. His dad also apologized and just kept asking "does Sharmane need anything?" At the time, I didn't realize that I needed counseling, but I do now. As an adult he came to me and asked me to forgive him and I told him that I already did.

Years went by and I graduated from high school and went to college. St. Augustine was great. I studied Forensics there. I started making friends and I met a guy from Brazil. We're going to call him Mike. We became friends and that was it. In college you experience things you never have before. Drinking was one of those things for me and many other students. It was just the thing to do in college. There were parties all the time. My girlfriends would drink and so I knew how to drink socially. One day Mike invited me to a party and everyone was drinking. I had a drink and sat it down to go to the bathroom. When I came back and drank from my cup, I felt dizzy and passed out minutes later. When I came back to consciousness, five different guys were taking turns raping me. I was afraid to tell anyone because they had already labeled me as a hoe even though I wasn't. This was a very traumatizing experience and as a result of it, I started to dislike men. When I finally got the courage to tell a friend on campus, she didn't believe me because the guys who gang raped me were all scholars. I went home for Christmas that year and did not want to return to school after the Christmas break. I still didn't tell my family that I had been assaulted. When my grandmother took me back to campus, I got a ride back to my hometown and stayed with friends until someone told my mom they saw me. At that point, I had to tell them what happened and why I decided to leave school. I didn't even get any of my things out of my dorm room. I was ashamed and angry that this had happened to me. I wouldn't wish that abuse on my worst enemy. My step father used to tell me if I drank at a party to never put my drink down and come back for it. Unfortunately, I did go back to it and it was spiked. Who would have thought someone would do that? These are things you see happening in movies, but this was my reality. My mom went and spoke to the dean and she told my mom that it does no one any good if I wouldn't tell her names of the guys who assaulted me. I asked, "what's the point when these are acclimated scholars who people at the school spoke highly of and looked up to?" It would be my word against theirs. I'd suffered enough embarrassment so I just wanted to leave and not show my face there again.

I now suffer from PTSD, manic depression, insomnia, and schizophrenia. I'm on medication to treat each, but at times, I feel like nothing helps me from reliving the things that have happened to me. Essentially, my whole outlook has changed towards men. I haven't found one who I can trust and that's a terrible feeling. I feel alone most of the time. I would love to find someone to love me but I'm afraid they will disappoint me. I've never had any counseling and I have lived a hard life, mostly by choice. It has been a downward spiral. It seems like I'm still fighting demons and I can't get a hold of things. My depression has made me withdraw from my loved ones, not because I don't want to be bothered, but because I don't want them to see me like this. Being sexually assaulted has taken a toll on me, as well as my mental health, but I will continue to pray for better days. I hope my story encourages someone else who has been molested or raped to tell someone so you can free yourself from the trauma and damage done to you.

Sharmane Burch *is a native of Whiteville, NC who now resides in Charlotte, NC. Sharmane loves to read, write short stories, and loves different types of music. She hopes to one day help other women speak up about being molested/raped by starting a support group for battered women.*

Facebook: Sharmane Burch

Scared to Tell

Ursula Jones

As old as I am today, I've still never told my parents I was molested by the babysitter as a child. I was scared to tell. I love my parents - God knows I do - but we couldn't tell things that happened in our house. Sometimes "our house" also meant other people's houses as well. The family business had to stay in the family. I don't know what would've happened if I even said anything. Lord bless the dead, my dad is gone now, and I never even tried to tell him. But my mom is here and the only way she will ever know this happened to me is if she reads this.
I'm going to share what I remember.

I grew up in a small town in Council, North Carolina. My parents raised my sisters and me right and they were always present in our lives. But just like most people, they had to work, so they needed a babysitter for us during the summer. My parents trusted my cousin from up north to come down and stay with us. She had to be about fifteen years old at the time and I was around nine. She grew up in a Christian home, just like us, so of course my parents considered that and thought she would be a good fit to keep us. Well, if they only knew she was on top of me in their bedroom every chance she got. She would make my sisters go to sleep and tell me to sleep in my parents' room when it was nap time. Then she would come in, lock the door and do her business. I wanted to tell my parents so badly but I couldn't. I was so brainwashed with the notion of whatever happens in the house stays in the house. It made me feel like I had to keep my mouth shut altogether. I also knew that it would be her word against mine. Who would ever think that your own family would do something like this to you? It's embarrassing to the family. I knew they would hate for me to even whisper a word.

I really don't know how my cousin had been raised behind closed doors. All I knew of her was that all her people who lived in Philly were in the church. Well miss little church cousin was in heat and picked me to molest. I don't know if she ever touched my siblings because I'm only telling what was done to me and I never asked them so as to not make them wonder. Not only did she molest me, she made me use the bathroom in a bucket on the front porch. We had two bathrooms but she wanted it in a bucket. She would even make me get in my dad's blue Duster. This car was a straight shift and as a little girl, I was scared of it. Well, I was pretty much scared of everything. Maybe that's why she targeted me, I'm not sure. But she would tell me to turn the gears for what made no sense to me at all. I don't know who tortured her as a child, but she came to NC and tortured me and I was scared to tell.

I couldn't wait for the summer to be over because the molestation was occurring every day and it was becoming like a norm. I was growing tired of having to put up with that mess on a daily. One day I thought to myself - *Is this life?* At a young age, this was happening to me and it was so sad I couldn't even go to my mom with this. Could you imagine how bad this hurt? It hurts knowing I couldn't go to my mom and tell her how I felt or what was going on with me. Now don't get me wrong, I love my mom and she loves me. But it's things that back in the day families would do that I would never do with my children. I always told my children as they were growing up that if anyone messed with them, no matter who it was, to tell me. After all that torture that happened to me as a child I would never want my children or grandchildren to ever hold anything.

The sad part about all of this is I really blocked it out of my mind as I began to get older. That is, until one day another cousin came down to visit like they would always do. By this time, I was grown with my own place. She came over to my house and we talked about everything to catch up on what had been going on in our lives because we stayed so far apart. Somehow I remember asking her about our cousin (the babysitter) who molested me and told her what happened that summer. She thought I made it up. She asked, "How can that be? Are you sure?" And I said "yes." She went on to tell me she was now an Evangelist. But my thing is, I don't care what she is now. What she did to me was real and she knows it. If I remember, I know she remembers. I've had to live with the memories of this trauma for years.

After that talk with my favorite cousin from Philly, I never spoke another word of it until last year. My best friend did a collaboration book and she told her story of how she too was molested as a child. After reading her story and knowing that it inspired others who have been molested, I knew I needed to tell my story too. My purpose for sharing is not to shame the family, but to encourage and help mothers to protect their children. I advise parents to listen to their children and ask questions and to watch who you leave your children with, whether it be family or friends. Love on your children and watch their body expressions. Do whatever you can to protect them from molestation.

Weeping may endure overnight, but there is joy in the morning. Psalm 30:5

Ursula Jones *is a native of Council, NC and currently resides in Lake Jackson, Texas. She is married to Ray Jones and is the mother of four beautiful children and six grandchildren. Ursula is the Founder and Owner of RJ Cleaning Services LLC, a Notary/Loan Signing Agent in the state of TX, and a 4X bestselling author. Ursula loves traveling, prioritizing her family, shopping and living life to the fullest. God is the head of her life and she knows through Him all things are possible. She trusts His plan for her life and allows Him to guide her footsteps to GREATER.*

Website: linktr.ee/prissyjvlogs

Acknowledgements

Tamla Eddington
Eddington's Tax Service
Facebook: Tamla Eddington
Instagram: @Tamla72

Stolen Virginity

Claudia Massey

"You'd better not ever tell anyone about this. Take it to your grave."

Those were the words my uncle uttered in my ear as he raped me. The first time it happened, I was about fifteen years old. He had called me back to his office one day. I never knew he drank, but his breath smelled like alcohol. He got so close to me and before I knew it, my small breasts were in his hands. I was shook and shocked. I couldn't move. What was he doing ? He's my uncle. He started acting aggressively saying "come here" while pulling and holding me closer. He pushed me to the desk as I tried to pull away crying, "NO! NO!!!" but he wouldn't stop! He was so forceful. My pants were coming down and before I knew it, he entered me.

I laid there.

Quiet.

Alone.
Afraid.
Hurt.
Disgusted.
Confused.

I felt so violated! My "UNCLE" just took my virginity. I didn't know about sex then. It didn't last long but knowing what I know now I believe he came inside of me and ate it out. Also, I know NOW he was small. Believe it or not, when he was done with me he gave me $100 like I was a prostitute. I walked out of the office and everyone was outside laughing and talking, living life to the fullest the way we knew it and I felt numb. Who would I tell? How could he do this to me – his own flesh and blood, a child? Of course I didn't have any expectations, but I certainly couldn't have foreseen this abuse occurring for years.

I grew up in a small country town called Council, just outside of Wilmington, North Carolina. Our town had one gas station, no stop lights and lots of fields. My uncle oversaw some of the largest lands in the town and as children, my cousins, brother and I worked for him in the tobacco fields during the summer. While I attribute my hard work ethic to my experience working in the fields, those same experiences unfolded a replica of lifelong trauma.

I thought I was receiving special treatment when I was taught how to drive the tractor. It got me out of cropping the tobacco. That "special treatment" came at a cost though, because it kept me closer to my uncle. He sexually abused me on the work bus, in his office and sometimes even in his home. Eventually, it became so routine that I became numb to it. I wanted so desperately for the abuse to end, but I didn't know how to make him stop.

My entire family was very close-knit. We always had large family cookouts, huge holiday gatherings and as Seventh-Day Adventists, attended church every Saturday. In fact, my family built our first and only Seventh-Day Adventist church in the town where my uncle served as a deacon for many years. My family was well-respected, my uncle being one of the most prominent of them all.

As a child, I was afraid to diminish that reputation. I feared no one believing me and casting me out of the family. When suffering abuse, especially as a child, one tends to fight, flight or freeze. Inevitably, I froze. I was stuck. I was surviving. Even as I write, I think as you are, Claudia, you could've said something or done something differently. Why didn't you kick him in his nuts? Why didn't you run out and tell everyone immediately? Why did you allow this to continue for so long? My answer is: I wasn't who I am today! I couldn't even think of these questions at that time. It's so easy for us to question a victim's actions and reactions, but please believe me, you don't know what you will do when you are traumatized. I lived with this day and night. I cried myself to sleep. So many times I would try to encourage myself to just walk down the hallway of our home and tell my mom but I couldn't do it. What would her reaction be? She loved her brother so much. He was very well known as a good Christian man. How could "I" taint that? I had nobody! Some days I was a walking zombie but smiling like I was the happiest person in the world.

I recall our church taking bus trips to other SDA churches to play basketball against each other. I was a cheerleader. Returning home from the games, it would be dark and I would sit with a boy who I was crushing on (being a teenager). My uncle would embarrass me and say "nothing better not be going on back there," - you know, like parents do. I thought how dare he. He was molesting me and God knows if I got pregnant, I would hope it wouldn't be from my old nasty uncle. The crazy thing is I loved my uncle. He is who we had for everything: My cousins and I looked up to him as well as his siblings. He had the money, he was head of our church, he had the businesses, he took us all on summer trips on the big bus (his bus). He was highly respected and the perfect candidate to be a predator because nobody would suspect him or it would be hard to believe.

They say children learn what they live and I believe it because he had a son to follow his footsteps and was also a predator. Yes, he raped me too and also told me to take it to my grave. My mom was the bookkeeper for my uncle's business. She was a single mom and needed the money. Sadly, I believe more often than less, children of single parents are more likely to be abused than those with a father in the home. There is no way my uncle would be comfortable enough to risk sexually assaulting me if he hadn't done it with other family members way before I was born. I maintained my distance as best I could and was thankful when school started back and we were no longer working in the fields during the summer.

Years of abuse led me to an early marriage as an escape away from the only life I had known. I was tired of being a slave to molestation and living life mute. I got married after high school. The abuse affected a lot of relationships because of my mindset. I've always been a beautiful girl, with a beautiful shape and I often wondered if that was the reason I was assaulted. Of course, as an adult now I know better. It had nothing to do with me; it was his mental illness. Yes, mental illness! You have to be sick to molest a child.

Being abused as a child, and especially by a family member, led me to be very protective over my children. As a single mother of three girls, I never let them spend the night with any of their friends. Their friends could only spend the night at our house and these sleepovers were far and few. I know they didn't understand it as children and they probably even thought I was being mean or too hard on them, but I was simply protecting them. I wanted to keep my girls as close to me as I could. My mom was the only one who watched them growing up while I went to work. It was very difficult for me to trust anymore. If my own uncle could molest me, his own niece, I knew a stranger wouldn't think twice about violating my babies. Of course, I also knew family was not excluded from the list of potential predators.

It wasn't until my mother passed in 2015 that I revealed what had happened to me. When I lost my mom, the family I loved all my life turned their backs on me. I had nobody and my emotions were all over the place. I didn't have anyone to protect anymore. I didn't have to carry the weight of this burden anymore. I've had nightmares for years. The chains were finally broken!

Shortly after, I discovered I wasn't the only one my uncle was molesting. Two of my cousins came forward and said the same was happening to them from a young age. We began to talk and share experiences and they were so similar. One of my cousins said the son (our cousin) took her virginity and told her he would kill her if she ever spoke a word. One of my cousins said when our uncle died in the 90's that she wanted to spit on his grave. He had so much power over her because she carried the trauma with her into her marriage and her everyday life.

I was threatened and told I better take it to my grave. Well, I didn't. The story is told and I pray it gives someone the strength to UNMUTE!! Talk Therapy with my cousins helped me heal. It helped all of us. We knew we were not alone. We finally had someone we could release to and who understood our pain. I wish we would've had one another during the time it was happening, but we were all scared children and knew our single moms needed their brother.

I'm a strong woman because I had to fight many battles in silence! Finally, I'm Unmuted from Molestation.

Claudia Massey *is a resident of Richmond, Virginia where she devotes much of her time being a wife to her husband, James, and a mother to their children. She is the mother of six daughters, three biological and three children who she adopted out of foster care. She is the Co-Founder of Patience for Patients, LLC, a non-medical homecare agency that provides personal care and companionship services to the geriatric population. Claudia attends Courthouse Road Church of Seventh-Day Adventists where she is a devoted member and Women's Ministry Leader. She is a Radio Host at Rejoice 101.3FM, a TV Host at Preach The Word Worldwide Network, a Certified Life and Wellness Coach, The Visionary Author of Amazon's #1 Best-Selling books, Reclaiming My Life and After the Storm, a recipient of The President Biden Lifetime Achievement Award and Host Ambassador for the state of Virginia, and a Columnist for Diva Dynasty Magazine. In her very spare time, she enjoys traveling with her family, feeding the homeless at local shelters and giving back to those in need through a family initiative she founded in memory of her mom, Rena's New Life Ministry. In November 2023, she will be releasing her documentary, Reclaiming My Life: The Claudia Massey Story.*

Facebook: @coachclaudiamassey
Instagram: @coachclaudiamassey
Website: claudiamassey.com

No More Closed Doors

Marcus Solomon

Imagine living in small town Farmers Union, North Carolina and having to be around your sexual abusers almost every day with a questionable witness and a clueless father. Well, that was my reality for six and a half years. I was living in a constant state of confusion and self-doubt and I had to find a way to get out. From the ages of four until 16, I had my innocence stripped of me. I was sexually assaulted by two of my male cousins. I can distinctly remember, even now 17 years later, the scent of their breath, their laundry detergent, the way my environment looked and smelled around me. I'm plagued with all of these horrid memories, in addition to bad dreams, major depression, suicidal thoughts, anxiety, as well as extreme panic attacks as a result of my assault with many years of healing ahead. The gut-wrenching experience of sexual molestation has left me with scars and trauma, some so deep that my brain has buried some of them to protect me. As a kid,

I was always labeled as different, feminine, or sweet. Years of bullying led to self-doubt, low self-esteem, and no confidence, which made me build a wall around my heart to protect it from any more damage.

While the latter years of my abuse are more vivid, while writing this, I actually recalled my very first assault, which happened at the age of four or five. My family and I lived in a terrible neighborhood in South Charlotte at the time and I can remember I had made friends with one of the kids in the neighborhood who was around my age. I would go over to his house and play and sometimes even eat dinner with his family. One night, the two of us were in his room and he pushed me over the bed and told me to pull my pants down. Without much thought, I pulled my pants down because, at that age, I didn't know it was wrong. That is, until I knew it was wrong. He began to try to penetrate me but was not able to. I can remember feeling his hard restricted area rubbing harshly against my backside. Thankfully, his father came walking down the hallway and he stopped and I ran behind the door to pull my pants up. I came from behind the door like it never happened and never spoke about it. Think about it: How does a four-year-old process that he was just sexually assaulted…by another four-year-old?

Then came (who we'll call) TJ, my second abuser. I was still around four or five around this time and it was the very first sleepover I had ever been to. All the cousins had come together at one of our Auntie's house like normal, but this night was different. After the nightly festivities were over and it was time to go to bed, we all made pallets on the floor to sleep on. I can remember TJ and I laying together under the same blanket. I felt his breath on my neck and his manhood pressed against the back of me. This was the first of many times. As I grew older, the assault got worse. It started with simple touches and gestures to eventually full intercourse. With the assaults becoming more common, I began to crave sex. I was sex driven.

The first time with K is still very faded in my head. I had been living with my dad, stepmom and step brother. This one was different - from growing up as brothers to now barely speaking, I guess the truth is too hard to bear. I can remember K's mom accusing me of sleeping with my younger cousin: "so you've slept with...?" My response left her speechless: "no, but I have been sleeping with your son." This was the beginning of a difficult weekend. My mom had come down to Whiteville, NC to visit and was staying at my sister's while she was here. So that Saturday morning my father and I went rabbit hunting and K came along later.

After the day of hunting was over, we went back home where K's mother and I began, or continued, a conversation. "I asked K if it was true and... he said yes. He said he wants you to go back where you came from," she said. My response was bold, "That's fine. It's not like my mom isn't down here anyway. I'll pack my bags and go." I then took my phone and was about to text my mom and let her know I would be coming back home with her. K's mom shouted "see that's your problem; you're always running your mouth, telling stuff! How about you tell some of your business. Tell what you're doing. Tell them how you're out here sleeping with boys." That's when she took her hand, put it around my neck and pushed me against the wall. "If this ever gets out, I'll make it look like it was you and not him," she said. All of this to a 16-year-old to protect her 19-year-old son who had been abusing me. All of this my father still does not know. What neither of them knew was that every time they went to the track, or to the "boom boom room", or wherever else they went, I was being sexually assaulted. As I got older and the assault got worse, I began to get shared between K and his cousins. They each at separate times penetrated me. I, afraid of my physical safety, kept all these secrets to myself until now.

Now you would think that as a 16-year-old, I would know and understand enough about sexual assault and molestation. However, it was not until I was 18 when I had a conversation with one of my aunts and I was describing to her what happened and she said, "Deuce, you've been sexually assaulted." In that moment, my abuse became reality. It's like the blinders came off my eyes and I was finally able to see the truth - my truth. All those years of being in turmoil, battling in my mind, and searching for an answer had finally made sense. I was a victim and was not afraid to say it.

This realization of what happened to me took an immediate toll on me. After coming to terms with the fact that I had been assaulted, I began to smoke marijuana to cope with the pain that I felt and the emotional strain from home. I also began using sex to deal with the emotions caused by the abuse. Now here I was doing something I said I would never do growing up: smoking every day just to get through and searching like a hound for the next guy I could get my hands on. I needed sex; it was the only thing that made me feel whole. The child inside was screaming for help but was not being heard. I grew up not feeling valued and sex became a coping mechanism for me. It was the only thing that made me feel valued, wanted. My young mind was altered into thinking my sexual assault was okay and I believed it was my fault.

These occurrences caused me to suffer from major anxiety and depression as well as suicidal thoughts. All throughout my high school experience I would have anxiety attacks, but I did not know what they were. I remember my heart beating uncontrollably, unsteady breathing, nauseousness, dizziness, intense sweating, and sometimes unexplainable crying as some of the effects of my attacks. I would walk around the hallways in high school in fear that someone was going to come and touch me from behind or pull me in the bathroom and molest me. As a result, I would always rush to the bathroom stalls to avoid urinals, take care of my business, and hurry out. These same fears have bled into college as well. Having communal bathrooms gives me chills. Having someone walk in the bathroom while I'm about to get in the shower makes me relive each moment like Déjà vu'.

I reached a point in my life where I was so overwhelmed with emotion that I had grown tired of living. I wanted to die. I could not find peace in life anymore. So, I planned to drive myself off the bridge on the way home from work one night. I can remember praying, "God, if you don't change my mind by the time I get off, I won't make it home tonight." I called one of my close friends crying because I promised her that no matter how hard life got, that I would continue to fight, but at that moment, I was tired. Tired of feeling worthless, constantly hiding in plain sight from the muted molestation of my mind, body, and soul. I knew that I needed help, I just was not sure where to get it yet.

That all changed when I started college. Once enrolled and on campus, I began searching for help. As first-year students, we were introduced to a lot of different staff members. I happened to be introduced to the head of counseling and knew exactly what I had to do. I asked myself, "how are you going to college to be a therapist when you need therapy?" So as soon as I could, I emailed the counseling services department and started intense weekly therapy. These sessions helped me reevaluate the truth about what happened in my life. They helped me unpack each box of trauma I hid in the crevices of my soul and allowed me to explore my faith deeper, experience God on a broader level while living in my truth. I was asked, "Marcus, why haven't you gone to God just as you are?" in a session one day and this question shook me to the core. My counselor was right; I had not gone to God with my trauma. I kept it bottled up on the inside while it ate at me for years. This question was life-changing, freeing me from the guilt of my past, years of beating myself up, blaming myself for my assault, and years of not knowing how to love myself properly. Therapy helped me rediscover the value in life again.

I'm sharing my journey, not only to help heal the inner child begging to be healed within me, but to help the next little boy or person who has experienced this same trauma. This is your sign that there is hope after the storm. I am proof that THERE IS GLORY AFTER THIS! Tell your story. Do not stay silent living in fear of what may happen. Free yourself! I was able to go through this healing journey with confidence through my faith, therapy, medication, and a small, dedicated support system. They helped me recover from the darkness around my heart, engulfed with deep wounds, waiting to be nurtured. I am now a student in college holding a Student Ambassador Position, a Shift Supervisor at work, while continuing to heal, grow, and discover new ways to love myself and everyone around me.

As I reflect on how much I have grown and the wonderful person I have become, I cannot take away from what got me to this point. Proverbs 3:5-6 says, "Trust in the Lord with all your heart, And lean not on your own understanding; In all your ways acknowledge Him, And He shall direct your paths" (NKJV). Every crooked path in my life, God has straightened out. Once I learned how to truly tap in and be honest with Him, I was able to open my heart up to be healed and that is exactly what is happening. Through every trial and tribulation, God has had His hand covering me, guiding me and ordering my every move. I pray that this will help free the next victim and save the lives of others.

Marcus Solomon *is from Farmers Union, North Carolina, but resides in Charlotte, NC with his mother and bonus father. He is a full-time student and is working towards maintaining a degree in Counseling and Human Services and Religion and Practical Theology, while minoring in English. He plans to continue his education and aspires to become a Licensed Clinical Mental Health Counselor, where he will focus on mental health, addiction, family, and marriage as well as staying an advocate for sexual assault. He also wants to build a school of arts. He believes that the next generation just needs someone to believe in them, help them find their voice, and strive for greatness.*

Facebook: Marcus Deuce Solomon
Instagram: @d.evoneee

Conclusion

Now that you've read this book, hopefully you have a clearer understanding of the impact of childhood molestation and the importance of protecting children. If you know of a child being molested, please speak up to a relative who is able to protect them or consider any of the resources below.

ChildHelpHotline.org
ChildWelfare.gov
Local Child Protective Services (CPS)

Made in the USA
Middletown, DE
12 September 2023

38139485R00029